NEAR-DEATH EXPERIENCES

CHRISTOPHER BAHN

CREATIVE EDUCATION • CREATIVE PAPERBACKS

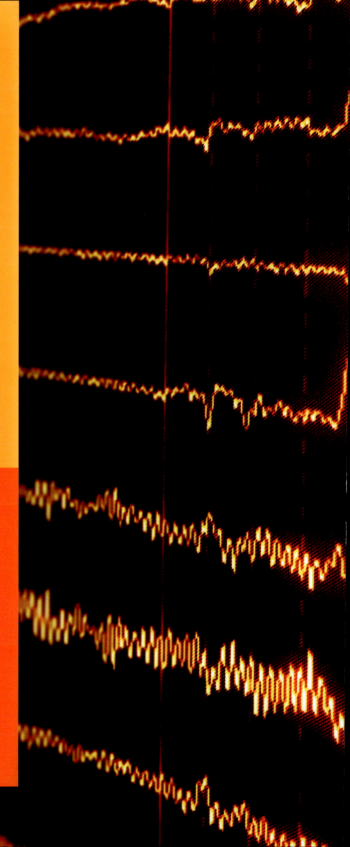

Published by Creative Education and Creative Paperbacks
P.O. Box 227, Mankato, Minnesota 56002
Creative Education and Creative Paperbacks
are imprints of The Creative Company
www.thecreativecompany.us

Design by Graham Morgan
Art direction by Blue Design (www.bluedes.com)

Images by Alamy Stock Photo/Deco, 4-5, Ian Allenden, 18, Shaun Wilkinson, 22; Getty Images/haydenbird, 37, montiannoowong, 20; Microsoft Designer/AI Generated, cover, 1; Shutterstock/agsandrew, 40, lassedesignen, 2, jurgenfr, 16, Taechit Tanantornanutra, 3, 48; Unsplash/Olga Kononenko, 41, Simon Godfrey, 43; Wikimedia Commons/Giovanni Francesco Romanelli, 39, Gower, Ronald, 45, Gustave Doré, 17, Hieronymus Bosch, 15, Leo Wehrli, 13, Luca Giordano, 44, Luigi Schiavonetti, 19, Luigi Schiavonetti/William Blake, 25, Michel Wolgemut, Wilhelm Pleydenwurff, 28, NASA, 31, Public Domain, 6, 30, 35, Public Domain/The Trustees of the British Museum, 11, Qiao Bin, 24, Raven Vasquez, 26, Thayer, Abbott Handerson, 8, Unbekannt, 12, Vasily Perov, 42, Wonderlane, 32

Every effort has been made to contact copyright holders for material reproduced in this book. Any omissions will be rectified in subsequent printings if notice is given to the publisher.

Copyright © 2025 Creative Education, Creative Paperbacks
International copyright reserved in all countries.
No part of this book may be reproduced in any form
without written permission from the publisher.

Library of Congress Cataloging-in-Publication Data
Names: Bahn, Christopher (Children's story writer) author.
Title: Near-death experiences / Christopher Bahn.
Description: Mankato, Minnesota : Creative Education, Creative Paperbacks, [2025] | Series: Enduring mysteries | Includes bibliographical references and index. | Audience: Ages 10–14 | Audience: Grades 7–9 | Summary: "An investigative approach to the mystery surrounding near-death experiences (NDEs) for age 12 and up, from historical accounts and popular myths to hard facts and evidence. Includes a glossary, index, sidebars, and further resources"—Provided by publisher.
Identifiers: LCCN 2024015976 (print) | LCCN 2024015977 (ebook) | ISBN 9798889892885 (library binding) | ISBN 9781682776544 (paperback) | ISBN 9798889893998 (ebook)
Subjects: LCSH: Near-death experiences—Juvenile literature.
Classification: LCC BF1045.N4 .B345 2025 (print) | LCC BF1045.N4 (ebook) | DDC 133.901/3—dc23/eng/20240510
LC record available at https://lccn.loc.gov/2024015976
LC ebook record available at https://lccn.loc.gov/2024015977

Printed in China

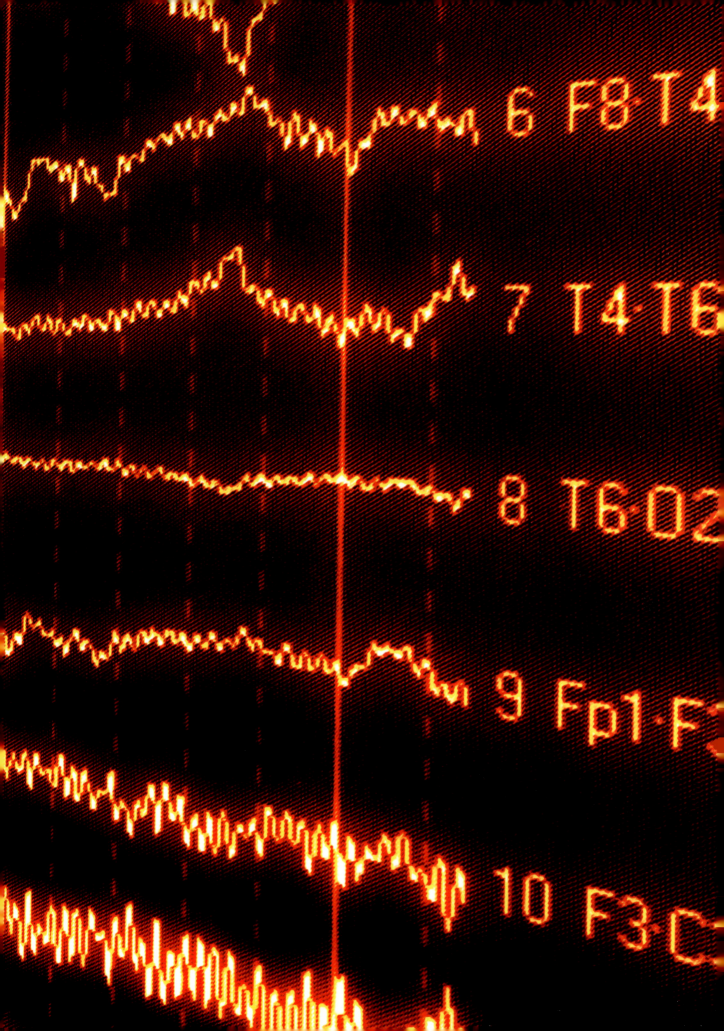

ULTIMOS MOMENTOS DE S. A. I.

A Senhora D. Maria Amélia de Bragança.

CONTENTS

Introduction 9

Describing the Indescribable 10

Trying to Make Sense 21

Famous Incidents 29

The Undiscovered Country 37

Field Notes 46

Selected Bibliography 47

Websites 47

Index 48

INTRODUCTION

Andrew was three and a half years old when he had open-heart surgery. About two weeks later, he asked his mother if he could go back to the beautiful place with all the flowers and animals. "I don't mean the park," he said. "I mean the sunny place I went to with the lady. . . . The lady that floats."

In the account described in Dr. Sam Parnia's book *What Happens When We Die*, Andrew told his mother he knew she was outside during his surgery. A year later, while watching a television show about open-heart surgery, Andrew recognized some of the machines. His mother told him he would not have seen any machines, because he'd been asleep during his operation. "I could see it when I was looking down," he insisted, "when I floated up with the lady." Later, when his mother showed him an old photo of *her* mother, Andrew's grandmother, who had died some time before, Andrew identified her as the floating lady. "It wasn't scary. It was lovely," he told his mother. "But I wanted to come back to see you." Andrew's mother came to believe that he had had a near-death experience.

OPPOSITE: Some near-death experience reports include seeing angels or deceased family members.

DESCRIBING THE INDESCRIBABLE

What happens after a person dies? Humans have wrestled with this question for thousands of years, and nobody has ever definitively answered it, though **philosophers**, doctors, priests, and poets have all tried. The playwright William Shakespeare called death "the undiscovered country" from which no traveler returns. Death is a one-way trip.

And yet there are some people who return from the brink of death with stories of what they've seen on the other side. These events are called near-death experiences (NDEs). In many ways, NDEs sound great. People report that they float in the air, feeling peaceful and happy. They're visited by loved ones who have died before them. Of course, there's a big problem: An NDE happens to a person who is so sick or injured that there is a significant chance they won't survive. In fact, they often seem so far gone that doctors think they already *have* died. That's

OPPOSITE: Shakespeare's tragic play *Hamlet* raises questions of what happens to people after they die.

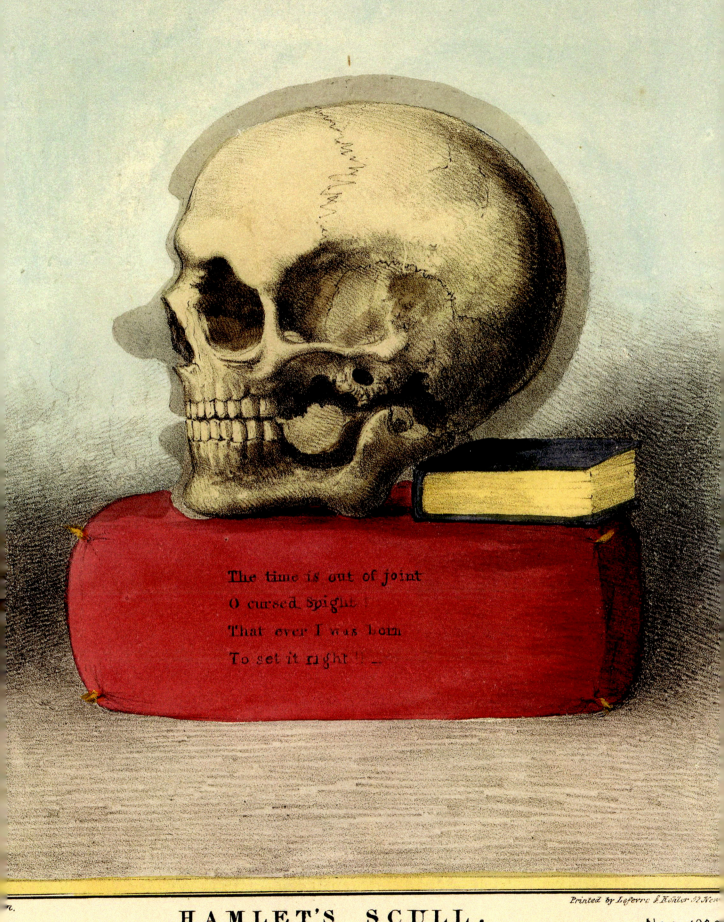

HAMLET'S SCULL.

"Why may not this be the Scull of some great Lawyer? where be his quiddets, and his quillets now? his cases, and his tricks? why suffer this disgrace? nor tell him of his actions of Battery; &c. &c.

Hamlet.

a big reason not much is known about NDEs: The only people who can describe them are those very close to dying.

Everything that lives must eventually die. In humans, doctors generally agree that death occurs when a person's heart or brain stop functioning, although this statement is complicated. For one thing, medical advances have sometimes allowed doctors to revive people who would have been considered irretrievably gone in earlier times. Questions about NDEs start with death. If a person's brain has stopped working, it would seem that they could not see or hear *anything*, let alone have the out-of-body sensations often reported. Other common NDE aspects, such as seeing what is happening in faraway places

OPPOSITE: Having experienced one firsthand, Albert Heim was a pioneer in the study of NDEs.

ALPINE HUT NAMED FOR ALBERT HEIM

or having conversations with long-dead relatives, are very strange indeed. These experiences are not possible, according to the current scientific understanding of the world. For this reason, some people dismiss NDE reports as **hallucinations** caused by medical trauma, or even deliberate **hoaxes** by people seeking attention or money.

NDEs have been discussed and debated for a very long time. Almost 2,500 years ago, Greek philosophers Plato and Democritus wrote about NDEs and tried to explain them using the science of their time. Dutch artist Hieronymus Bosch's painting *Ascent of the Blessed*, created between 1505 and 1515, shows spirits of the recently dead being guided into heaven by winged angels who fly them into a tunnel of light. Such luminous tunnels are commonly reported by NDE survivors. Swiss geologist and mountain climber Albert Heim (1849–1937) had an NDE when he was almost killed in a climbing accident. He wrote that he experienced "a great, glorious moment" in which he felt himself rising from the earth as powerful chords of organ music played around him. He collected tales of similar episodes from 30 climbers, soldiers, and others and published them in 1892. Heim's collection is considered one of the first scientific works on NDEs.

For much of the 20th century, incidents such as these were examined primarily by philosophers and those who studied religious faith and beliefs. NDEs are still often claimed as proof that God exists. But NDEs also raise important questions about consciousness—that

DESCRIBING THE INDESCRIBABLE

13

> **OPPOSITE:** NDEs may include visions of an afterlife and a feeling of weightlessness.

is, the way the mind understands a person's self and their place in the world around them. Consciousness is like a computer program running in the background of a person's brain. It gathers and interprets sensory input, accesses a person's memories, and creates a sense of past and future. It also produces emotions, **morality**, creativity, and personality.

How does the brain *create* consciousness? What are the physical processes that control it? And how does near-death affect this all-important part of being human? Some regard consciousness as the human soul, and that raises another question that science may never be able to answer: Does a person truly have a soul that exists outside of the body, or is consciousness entirely created by our physical brain? Is there some part of a human being that keeps on going after the body dies—an intangible spirit or soul? Where does it go? And how does it get there?

In the 1970s, scientists began to look at NDEs in a more serious way. They were interested in how people whose brains had stopped working were apparently able to remember events. How could they hear and see things going on around their body, as they claimed? **Psychologists** were interested in what NDEs might reveal about death and dying. They were also interested in how these experiences could dramatically change a survivor's personality.

Raymond Moody, a **psychiatrist**, coined the term "near-death experience" in his 1975 book *Life after Life*. Moody interviewed about 150 people about strange experiences they'd had while on the verge of death. Their stories were remarkably similar. Another psychiatrist

NEAR-NEAR-DEATH EXPERIENCES

Psychiatrist Raymond Moody describes a variant form of an NDE he calls a "shared death experience." People *near* the dying person report uncanny events at the moment of death. Moody says these bystanders, who are not near death themselves, may see ghosts of the dying person or their deceased loved ones, hear strange music, or even feel themselves leave their own bodies or witness a life review of the deceased. Moody says he doesn't know how many shared-death experiences there have been but insists they are more common than is generally realized. In 2012, two Italian **neurologists** wrote that one of their patients had experienced an NDE-like event when he wasn't even dying, just emotionally upset. The man suddenly saw a "great white light" and was filled with a profound feeling of love and joy. The experience seemed to happen spontaneously. Others have reported suddenly knowing that a loved one had died at that very moment, even thousands of miles away. Unfortunately, shared-death experiences are even less understood than NDEs, so whatever they are—a message from beyond or just an uncanny coincidence—remains a mystery.

and NDE researcher, Bruce Greyson, identified about 15 common themes. These themes helped create the Greyson Scale, a way of measuring NDE reports that is still in use today. The most common elements include:

- A sensation of leaving the body
- An unusual clarity of mind
- A sense of traveling into a tunnel, or into darkness
- Bright light
- A sense of peace and love
- A sense of having access to unlimited knowledge
- A "life review" of important past events, like "having your life flash before your eyes"
- A preview of the future
- Visits from loved ones who are already dead, or other beings of a religious or otherworldly nature

No NDE is exactly the same. Not every element on the Greyson Scale occurs every time. And as far as researchers know, not everyone near death has an NDE. But a surprisingly large number of people say they have—as many as 9 to 18 million Americans, according to surveys, and recent research shows NDE reports among 23 percent of heart-attack survivors. NDEs have been reported by people from nearly all countries and cultures, all age groups, and all gender identities. Going back into ancient history,

17

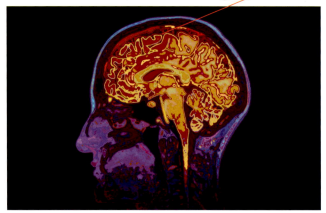

MEDICAL IMAGE OF A HUMAN BRAIN

scholars find stories of NDEs in the cultures of Egypt, India, China, and Central America.

For some people, NDEs are proof of some form of religious or spiritual afterlife and a caring God who watches over people. This is the view of Dr. Jeffrey Long, a Kentucky physician who founded the Near-Death Experience Research Foundation (NDERF) in 1998. The NDERF website has collected more than 5,000 NDE reports in 30 languages. Long describes the typical NDE as profoundly beautiful and comforting, showing that death itself is not to be feared. "Death isn't the end," Long has said. "I'm convinced that we're all going to be back together again some day in a very, very beautiful afterlife."

Others are more **skeptical**, such as Chris French, head of the Anomalistic Psychology Research Unit at the University of London. He takes the position that **paranormal** explanations for NDEs should be treated as extremely unlikely. He stresses that physical and psychological causes must be investigated thoroughly first. To French and scientists like him, NDEs are likely creations of a brain that is struggling with injury, loss of oxygen, or chemical imbalances. NDEs can't be predicted. There is no way to know when someone will experience one. This makes them difficult to study. It also means that NDEs can't be understood or tracked in the way a heartbeat can. As a result, many medical researchers don't take them seriously or, at the least, aren't convinced there is a good way to examine them scientifically. Not yet, anyway. With advances in technology, the search goes on to figure out what NDEs are, what causes them, and what might be learned from them.

A DEPARTING "SOUL"

TRYING TO MAKE SENSE

OPPOSITE: In most NDEs, religious imagery, such as this Buddha, is directly tied to the person's culture.

People who've had an NDE insist NDEs are as real as any other experience. While nobody denies that NDE survivors did experience something, the fact that it literally seems to happen out of this world makes it very hard to examine. Many religions and spiritual traditions teach that humans have a soul that exists independently of the physical body, and this soul supposedly travels to another place when the body dies—the afterlife. A school of philosophy called materialism disagrees. It says the only real things are those that can be measured and examined and obey the known physical laws of science. A materialist would say there is no soul or afterlife, and any perception otherwise during an NDE must be an illusion.

So, NDEs present scientists with a dilemma: Millions of people have reported having an NDE, but science cannot study something for which there is no physical evidence. Many stories have been collected, but

OPPOSITE: Movement toward a bright light is often part of an NDE.

even with advances in technology, scientists have not yet been able to put some of the most bizarre-sounding aspects of NDEs to the test.

Scientists and philosophers work to expand human knowledge of life and the universe through a process known as the scientific method. In its simplest terms, this means being skeptical but non-judgmental of any explanation for why something happens until that explanation has been tested. This is the basis of all science. It's also a good basis for logical thinking. But as space scientist Carl Sagan once said, "extraordinary claims require extraordinary evidence." Any claims involving the miraculous or supernatural are, by Sagan's definition, extraordinary—which is not to say they should be automatically dismissed. Despite the increasing scientific attention to NDEs, their study is still new. It is very much an open question whether there is a supernatural or religious explanation for NDEs, or if they are simply an illusion caused by oxygen starvation or the other processes that happen to the human body close to death. If NDEs are real, does that definitely mean there is life after death? Not necessarily. It's one possible interpretation of the evidence, say many researchers, but it is an extraordinary claim—one that requires extraordinary proof.

One common question about NDEs is whether they are experienced differently by people from different countries and cultures. A team of Iranian scientists writing in the journal *Frontiers in Psychology* in 2023 analyzed more than 2,400 NDE reports from around the world. They found a "common core" among all respondents, including the elements described by Moody and Greyson, such as out-of-body experiences. "This is what all ethnic groups and nations face," they wrote, "without exception and without being influenced by religion, race, culture, and the native customs of their countries." But they also found that NDEs include

OPPOSITE: An etching from Robert Blair's poem "The Grave" based on a watercolor by William Blake

symbols and imagery "rooted in the personal archive" of the experiencer and important only to them. This supports earlier findings by Greyson and others that NDE survivors see visions related to their own cultural background. For example, a Christian might see Jesus, a Buddhist might see Buddha, and a Hindu might see Krishna. The meaning of this is inconclusive. Skeptics note that if the brain does imagine the NDE, it would be unlikely to show a person a vision of something they weren't already familiar with. Chris French notes, "What people experience reflects their own cultural background. For example, Christians never meet Hindu gods during near-death experiences—but people from all cultures can experience NDEs." But Jeffrey Long says that the differences are small and not what's important. "It doesn't matter whether you're a Muslim in Egypt, a Hindu in India, or a Christian in the United States. What you experience will be strikingly similar."

Experts have also found that NDEs cannot be fully explained by some similar **phenomena**. For example, NDEs are not strictly out-of-body experiences, which can happen to people with **epilepsy** or brain injuries or as a result of exposure to some drugs. While out-of-body experiences are a regular feature of NDEs, they more often occur when people are *not* near death. Scientists have also created out-of-body experiences in the laboratory by direct electrical stimulation of people's brains. But out-of-body experiences lack many of the features of NDEs, such as life reviews or meetings with deceased loved ones. And although some scientists think NDEs are a form of hallucination, they are not the same kind often caused by mind-altering drugs or

DEATH OF THE BUDDHA

powerful painkillers. NDE experts note that drugs generally cloud people's thought processes, including memory, whereas NDEs make perceptions vivid and memorable. NDEs are not simply dreams, either. People usually forget their dreams. Dreams they do remember typically do not affect daily routines.

In any case, NDEs can be life-altering. Whether NDEs are religious experiences or not, survivors are often profoundly changed afterward. This can be positive, resulting in greater empathy for others, calmness, and renewed purpose in life. Many NDE survivors are moved to change their lives and the world around them for the better. Some find work in fields where they help others. They may go to work in end-of-life (hospice) facilities, comforting those who are facing their own deaths.

However, many NDE survivors also feel lost and adrift, unsure where they fit into the world after going through such an event. Some are troubled by an inability to describe what they saw. Others worry that if they share their story, people will think they're mentally ill. Many NDE survivors suffer depression afterward, regretting that they were pulled back to their familiar lives. Author P. M. H. Atwater, writing on

MUSIC FROM BEYOND

Many NDE survivors have personality changes or discover new life interests. Surgeon Anthony Cicoria was struck by lightning at a family picnic in 1994. He remembers being pushed forward out of his body, which he looked down on with astonishment. "I'm dead," he remembers thinking. He felt himself dissolve into a ball of light, along with an overwhelming sense of peace. Suddenly, he reawakened to discover that he had been given life-saving measures. He was alive again. And something more: When Cicoria recovered, he was overcome with a passion for music. He learned to play the piano, obsessively practicing for hours. He would get up at 4:00 a.m. and play before work, then past midnight afterward. He began composing his own music, which came to him in endless waves of inspiration. Cicoria's dramatic life changes were not all positive, however. He began taking unwise physical risks and was injured in a motorcycle accident. His marriage also collapsed, due in large part to his personality change. Cicoria's newfound musical talent is an example of "acquired savant sydrome," in which a person develops extremely advanced insights or abilities after an injury or disease.

the website of the International Association for Near-Death Studies (IANDS), says that a post-NDE personality change, even into someone kinder and nicer, may be unnerving to friends and family who do not recognize the new person. A renewed interest in religion may alienate those unready or unwilling to join the person on their new path. Researchers have found that NDEs are also hard on marriages. Survivors' spouses may come to think of them as strangers. Not surprisingly, researchers report an extremely high divorce rate among NDE survivors—65 percent or more. NDEs may also be hard for young people. In her research, Atwater found high rates of suicide, depression, and alcoholism among adults who had NDEs as children.

Even one mostly positive aspect of an NDE, the loss of the fear of death, has its dark side. NDE survivors sometimes become risk-takers in a way that may seem foolhardy or dangerous to others. The writer Ernest Hemingway was deeply affected in this way by his NDE during World War I (1914–18). And after a man named Anthony Cicoria survived a lightning strike that gave him an NDE, he later nearly died again in two different motor-vehicle accidents. "I'm not afraid of death," he said. "I take it to the edge."

Several NDE researchers, including Atwater, Bruce Greyson, and retired University of Connecticut psychology professor Kenneth Ring, have also written that NDEs can be a mystical event that can grant survivors newfound special powers. These may include visions of future events and continued contact with the spiritual guides met during the NDE itself. Stories of paranormal abilities, however, are exactly what Carl Sagan meant by "extraordinary claims." Others have been very skeptical, such as Michael N. Marsh, a medical researcher who also studied religious faith and beliefs at the University of Oxford. He wrote in 2016, "It is amazing what some people believe."

FAMOUS INCIDENTS

Stories about NDEs have been around for a long time. One of the earliest comes from Plato, the ancient Greek philosopher who wrote a famous work called *The Republic* 2,400 years ago. In it, he discusses a soldier named Er who died in battle but woke up just before being cremated. Er spoke of visiting a place where the spirits of the recently dead were judged and offered new lives back on Earth. The oldest known medical description of an NDE was written in 1740 by Pierre-Jean du Monchaux, a French physician. He reported that a patient dying from blood loss said later that he saw a bright light that seemed to be heaven.

Many such stories have been told throughout history. They often suggest that people's souls go on to another life after they die. In many beliefs, from Christianity to Buddhism to Egyptian mythology, it's told that the dead stop first at a place of judgment, where their performance in this life is suitably rewarded or punished. Not all NDE tales have

OPPOSITE: Plato also wrote about the legendary lost underwater city of Atlantis.

29

OPPOSITE: Leaving one's body and viewing a room, a city, or even the planet from above has been reported during NDEs.

that element of final judgment. One involved British Admiral Francis Beaufort, remembered today for his scale for measuring winds. At the beginning of his naval career, he fell off a boat in Portsmouth Harbor. He didn't know how to swim. Years later, Beaufort wrote of struggling in the water and sinking from exhaustion. Then he was overcome by calmness, after which every scene of his life appeared to him at once, "in a kind of panoramic view."

Carl Jung was one of the world's most influential psychiatrists and scholars. He studied spirituality and stressed that it was an essential part of human life. In 1944, following a heart attack, Jung had what many regard as an NDE. In his autobiography, he described seeing Earth from space. He floated to a temple like ones he had seen in Sri Lanka. There, he painfully had "the whole phantasmagoria of earthly existence . . . stripped from [him]," until only his essential self remained and he felt a "great fullness." When his doctor appeared before him, they communicated without speaking; the doctor told Jung he had to return to Earth. Jung was disappointed but also worried for his doctor, because Jung felt that his appearance during Jung's NDE meant that he was *also* near death. And indeed, wrote Jung, the man died of blood poisoning soon afterward.

Pim van Lommel is a former heart doctor and NDE researcher from the Netherlands. He documented a famous case of a man found in a coma in a park. When the man was taken to the hospital, he had no pulse. He was not breathing. He had no blood pressure and no brain reflexes. Even so, doctors and nurses worked for 90 minutes to **resuscitate** him. A nurse took out his false teeth and put them in a drawer. A week later, the man emerged from his coma. "That nurse

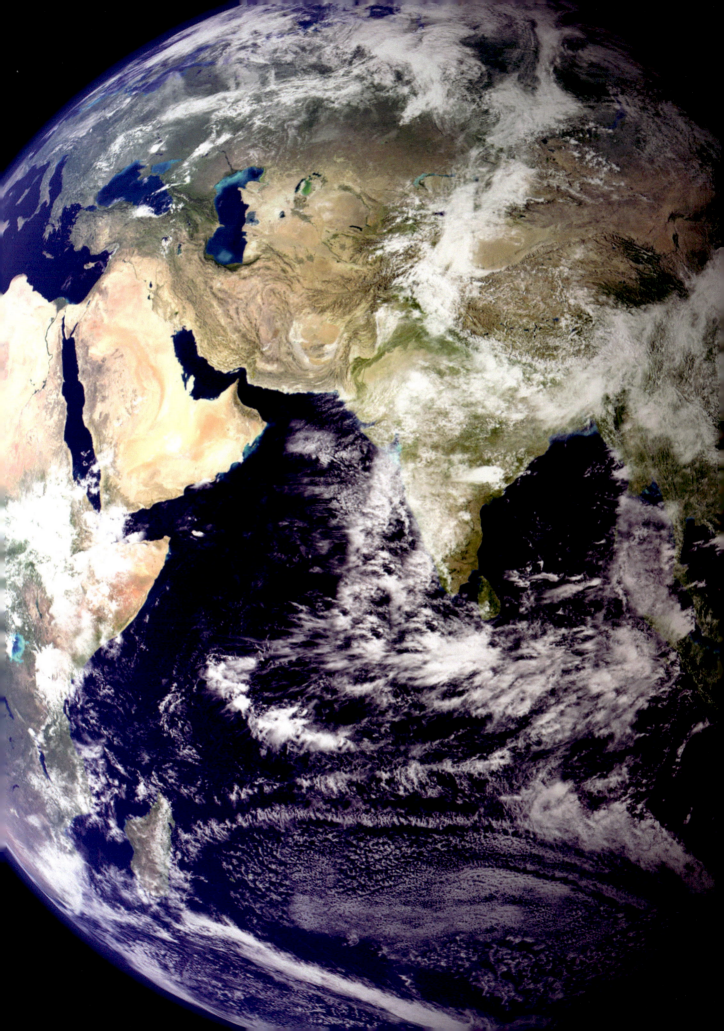

IN BETWEEN

In Buddhist belief, people enter a state called the bardo when they die. This is a middle state between one life and the next, when the dead person is reincarnated, or reborn, in a new life on Earth. The bardo has features similar to those of an NDE. It features three main stages. The "painful bardo of dying" begins when the body begins to sicken and ends with death. In the "luminous bardo of dharmata," the body is left behind, and the person is left with nothing but mind and **meditation**. This stage is filled with bright light, and the deceased is confronted by peaceful and wrathful gods who guide them toward nirvana, beyond the cycle of reincarnation and the final goal of existence. However, if the person has not yet achieved enlightenment, they are guided back to Earth to try again in another cycle of reincarnation. They undergo the "karmic bardo of becoming," reemerging in a new body. Buddhists believe life on Earth is important because it offers the opportunity to advance spiritually. Those with good karma, such as thoughtful and compassionate people, are granted a more fortunate rebirth.

knows where my dentures are," the man said, pointing to the nurse. He said she had put them in a sliding drawer in a cart. The man said he had witnessed the resuscitation efforts and had been afraid that they might stop. He told doctors he had tried to make them aware that he was not dead. His dentures were found right where he said the nurse had put them.

Journalist Sebastian Junger's NDE, which happened when he ruptured an artery in 2020, was both frightening and inspirational. He says that as he passed out in the operating room, "a black pit opened up underneath me and I felt myself being pulled into the pit." He then felt the "essence" of his father welcoming him. As someone who doesn't believe in God, Junger says that even after his experience he doesn't believe in an afterlife. He does think it's possible, though, that reality interacts with "some kind of energy or quantum phenomena" as yet unknown.

Randy Schiefer told his NDE story to National Public Radio in 2022. He said that after going into a coma due to an infectious disease called COVID-19, he traveled through a light-filled tunnel. It brought him to a large room filled with stained glass, beyond which was a "golden city" he called "absolutely stunning." There, he met a mysterious man who told him he did not belong and had to leave. Schiefer says he panicked and began to cry, not knowing where he was or how to leave, but he was guided back to consciousness by someone who called him by name. Schiefer says he is no longer afraid of death, and his lifelong panic attacks have stopped.

In 2023, pop singer Madonna had an NDE after being in a coma for four days due to a bacterial infection. She said it felt as though God asked her to "come with" him, at which point she awoke and said her first word aloud: "No."

Some NDE accounts have been turned into books and movies. Several became best-sellers for Christian publishing houses in the early 2010s. One was *Heaven Is for Real*, the story of a three-year-old boy's NDE during emergency surgery. It was cowritten by the boy's father, a Nebraska minister. It tells how the boy, Colton Burpo, met his late great-grandfather, as well as an unborn sister his parents had never told him about. Colton also said he met several important Christian figures, including John the Baptist and Jesus, who rode a rainbow-colored horse. The book sold more than 10 million copies and was made into a movie in 2014.

Another book, *The Boy Who Came Back from Heaven*, had a more negative reception. It was written by the father of Alex Malarkey, a six-year-old boy who was in a car accident. Alex was permanently paralyzed and in a coma for two months. He told his parents that during his NDE, he had seen angels and met Jesus. But in 2015, 11 years later, Alex said the entire story was false. He'd made up the story to get attention, and his father had added details to it. The publisher stopped printing the book, which had sold one million copies.

Both NDE books drew criticism from other Christians. One was John MacArthur, an influential **evangelical** pastor. "All these supposed trips to heaven are hoaxes, and they prey on people in the most vulnerable way, because they treat death in a superficial, deceptive fashion," he told the *Guardian* news magazine.

In any case, NDEs are a frequent theme in fiction. Writer Ernest Hemingway was badly wounded during World War I. He said he felt his soul slip away "like you'd pull a silk handkerchief out of a pocket. . . . It flew all around and then came back and went in again, and I wasn't dead

Writer Ernest Hemingway had an NDE after being wounded in Italy in 1918.

anymore." He adapted his vision of death into the story "The Snows of Kilimanjaro." In it, a dying man lost in the jungle is rescued by a pilot who flies them into a storm, after which they emerge into a peaceful white light high in the sky—and perhaps the afterlife. In J. R. R. Tolkien's *The Lord of the Rings*, the wizard Gandalf is killed and revived after a fierce battle, telling his friends of a land awaiting after death with "white shores, and beyond, a far green country under a swift sunrise." A more Buddhist take on NDEs is found in George Saunders's 2017 novel, *Lincoln in the Bardo*. In the story, the 11-year-old son of U.S. president Abraham Lincoln, after dying of typhoid fever, encounters other dead spirits in the bardo, a place between death and rebirth.

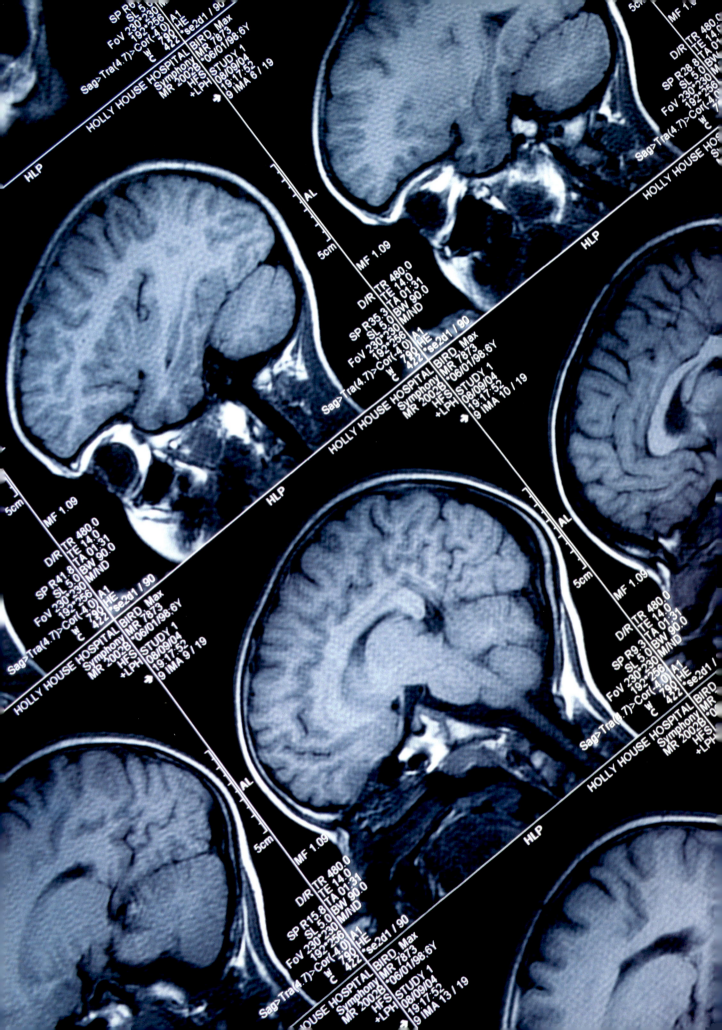

THE UNDISCOVERED COUNTRY

OPPOSITE: Advances in technology can help detect subtle physical changes in the human brain during an NDE.

Not long ago, many scientists considered NDEs to be a fringe belief, not much different from Bigfoot or UFOs. But the past few decades have seen a big shift. NDEs are becoming an accepted area of scientific research. Dr. Kevin Nelson, a University of Kentucky neurologist and author of the book *The Spiritual Doorway in the Brain*, said in 2015 that evidence for NDEs is as strong as "germ theory of disease and evolution stand in other branches of science." It is still far from clear exactly what happens in an NDE. But increasingly, the evidence suggests that NDEs really do occur. "They may be true. They may be false," said brain scientist Christof Koch in 2022. "But the fact that we do have experiences—that is the remarkable thing."

OPPOSITE: A feeling of peace and comfort during an NDE is often reported by survivors.

It is extremely difficult to study NDEs. It would be unethical and dangerous to recreate them in the laboratory. When they happen to people outside the lab, doctors are often far more interested in saving lives than documenting visions of the afterworld. Dr. Sam Parnia, an associate professor of medicine at NYU Langone Health, says that learning more about when and how the moment of death happens could lead to big advances in medical techniques for saving people's lives.

Parnia's team has been running an ongoing study of NDEs during heart attacks called AWARE (AWAreness during REsuscitation), which has examined more than 500 heart patients at 25 hospitals in the United States and the United Kingdom. In 2019, the team interviewed a group of heart-attack survivors. They reported that 19 percent of the survivors had experienced memories of the event, including feelings of peace and joy, visits from relatives, and images of what was happening around them while they were unconscious. In 2023, the team reported that the brains of some heart-attack patients who had been clinically dead for up to an hour burst into a jolt of electrical activity when life-saving measures were performed. Parnia's team also tested the idea that people can see the room around them during an NDE. Without interfering with patients' emergency treatment, team members measured patients' brainwaves and displayed video and audio cues such as the repeated words *apple, pear, banana*. None of the 28 survivors later correctly identified the video cue, and only one picked the right fruit. That's no better than random chance, some critics have noted. Still, Parnia says the AWARE-II results show that what he calls the "**lucid**, hyper-conscious experience" of NDE is real. His team's study suggests that the dying brain turns off certain systems

ENDURING MYSTERIES | NEAR-DEATH EXPERIENCES

38

that normally prevent such visions, which, they say, may open access to "new dimensions of reality."

Parnia's study isn't the only example of NDEs producing uncanny effects in the brain. In their book *Mindsight*, psychologists Kenneth Ring and Sharon Cooper discuss 21 cases of blind NDE survivors who report being able to see during the experience. Ring has suggested that this is a form of "transcendental awareness" that may not truly be sight but, rather, something interpreted that way by the brain.

Kevin Nelson, who has studied the relationship between NDEs and dreams, believes that many of the features of NDEs can be explained as the brain going into a hybrid state between wakefulness and dreaming. Nelson says that the physiological experiences of dreaming and NDEs are very similar. The sensations and visions people have during an NDE may be no more real than that of a dream, although it "may deeply touch someone's impression of reality." He adds that examining NDEs scientifically does not mean there isn't also a spiritual meaning behind them.

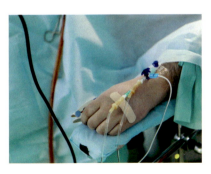

NDEs are unusual in that the memory they create tends not to fade away as other kinds of trauma do. Experiencers can often still vividly recall them in detail years later. Altered perceptions may be an effect of the brain attempting to survive through a medical crisis such as a heart attack. The lack of blood flow may cause a person's consciousness to fade in and out, and that on-and-off condition might make a person incorrectly seem to be unconscious or even dead, but actually be at least partly aware of what's happening around them. There is also evidence that even people in a deep coma may be able to sense external events, such as people talking to them. Out-of-body experiences are a common part of NDEs,

FYODOR DOSTOYEVSKY

but Nelson notes that they can also occur during dreams and can be artificially induced by electrically stimulating the brain.

Low doses of the hallucinogenic drug DMT have been shown to produce effects very similar to NDEs. In 2019, researchers from the University of Michigan discovered that the brains of rats produce floods of DMT at the moment of death. It is possible that this also happens in humans, thus explaining the hallucinatory-seeming effects of NDEs.

Scientists researching epilepsy in Estonia in 2022 were recording a patient's brainwaves when he unexpectedly died of a heart attack. By accident, the scientists had recorded what was happening in his brain at the moment of his death. The patterns they recorded are usually associated with dreaming and memory, suggesting that the dying brain might replay important life events one last time—exactly what NDE reporters claim. NDEs share other similarities with epileptic attacks. Russian novelist Fyodor Dostoyevsky (1821–81), who suffered from epilepsy, wrote that his fits often made him feel a sensation of deep joy and harmony. Modern brain surgeons can reproduce this by stimulating a specific region of a person's brain with electricity, producing **euphoria** and an out-of-body effect. This could be the first step in recreating an NDE in safe laboratory conditions.

Stories about an afterlife are common to all human cultures and have existed for thousands of years. Religions and philosophers have tried to help humans understand and come to terms with death and

MOMENTS OF CLARITY

The unusual clarity that many NDE survivors report, such as seeing surprisingly vivid colors and lights, might be related to a similarly strange and little-understood phenomenon that sometimes happens to people with terminal illnesses just before they die. This rare event has been reported since at least the 19th century. It was given the name "terminal lucidity" in 2009 by Michael Nahm, a German NDE researcher. Terminal lucidity has been observed by doctors when dying patients suddenly and inexplicably rally and go through an energy surge. The patients, who often suffer from severe conditions such Alzheimer's disease, become more alert, able to speak and move, and remember memories that they had been unable to just prior to the rally. This can be both positive and negative for the patients and their loved ones. It may be confusing or distressing and may lead to unrealistic hopes that a full recovery will happen. But it can also give people an unexpected opportunity to say goodbye before the final approach of death.

what, if anything, awaits people afterward, in books such as the Bible and the Koran. Interestingly, NDEs seem to be just as likely to occur to people who do not believe in God as to religious believers.

So far, NDEs do not actually explain very much about what awaits people after death, usually only showing the first minute or so and the merest glimpses or hints of what lies beyond that. If eternity is a grand hotel, NDEs seem to show only the lobby. The dark threshold between life and death is one of the least understood in all of human experience. And yet death is also the one experience that everyone on Earth is guaranteed to have. Understanding death is one of the most profound questions there is. Finding even a partial answer to any aspect of it might help save lives. It might also improve the quality of life for those nearing death and ease their transition from this world into whatever comes next.

Whether an NDE is a genuine vision of the afterlife or just a dream-state flooding the dying brain—or both—is still open to inquiry. Raymond Moody, speaking in 2023 to the New York Academy of Sciences, noted that NDEs may be impossible to ever fully understand. "I think the questions that we are dealing with—a lot of them are not yet scientific questions. I think they are philosophical questions." Perhaps nobody has expressed this idea better than William Shakespeare's character Hamlet, as he mused about the possibility of life after death: *To sleep, perchance to dream: ay, there's the rub—for in that sleep of death, what dreams may come?*

FIELD NOTES

epilepsy—a neurological disorder most often marked by seizures

euphoria—a feeling of intense confidence, happiness, and well-being

evangelical—belonging to a tradition within Protestant Christianity that emphasizes belief in the Bible as being the true word of God and a personal conversion to faith

hallucination—a physical perception of things that do not exist outside the mind

hoax—a humorous or harmful deception; a trick

lucid—clear and intelligible

meditation—thinking deeply or concentrating on an idea, sound, or image in order to clear one's mind of distractions

morality—good conduct, or a system of rules or values for good conduct

neurologist—a doctor or medical specialist who works with the brain and nervous system

paranormal—events or phenomena which are beyond current scientific explanation, such as telepathy or ghosts

phenomenon—an occurrence that can be observed

philosopher—a person who examines or develops systems of beliefs

psychiatrist—a doctor who diagnoses and treats mental illnesses

psychologist—a person who studies the mind and its functions

resuscitate—to revive from death or unconsciousness

skeptical—doubtful or questioning

SELECTED BIBLIOGRAPHY

Atwater, P. M. H. *The Big Book of Near-Death Experiences: The Ultimate Guide to What Happens When We Die.* Charlottesville, Va.: Hampton Roads, 2007.

Bachrach, Judy. *Glimpsing Heaven: The Stories and Science of Life after Death.* Washington, D.C.: National Geographic, 2014.

Greyson, Bruce. *After: A Doctor Explores What Near-Death Experiences Reveal about Life and Beyond.* New York: St. Martin's Essentials, 2021.

Hashemi, Amirhossein, et al. "Explanation of Near-Death Experiences: A Systematic Analysis of Case Reports and Qualitative Research." *Frontiers in Psychology,* April 19, 2023. https://www.frontiersin.org/journals/psychology/articles/10.3389/fpsyg.2023.1048929/full

Nelson, Kevin. *The Spiritual Doorway in the Brain: A Neurologist's Search for the God Experience.* New York: Dutton, 2011.

Parnia, Sam. *What Happens When We Die: A Groundbreaking Study into the Nature of Life and Death.* Carlsbad, Calif.: Hay House, 2006.

WEBSITES

International Association for Near-Death Studies
https://www.iands.org
Explore articles, videos, and other resources from this nonprofit organization.

Near-Death Experience Research Foundation
http://www.nderf.org
Read true stories and FAQs related to near-death experiences.

INDEX

Atwater, P. M. H., 25, 27
bardo, 32, 35
Beaufort, Francis, 30
Boy Who Came Back from Heaven, The, 34
brains, human, 12, 14, 18, 24, 37, 38, 40, 41, 42, 45
Burpo, Colton, 34
Cicoria, Anthony, 26, 27
common elements
  afterlife, 18, 21, 29, 33, 35, 42, 45
  angels, 9, 13, 17, 34
  clarity, 17, 25, 43
  deceased family members, 9, 10, 13, 16, 17, 24, 33, 34, 38
  floating, 9, 10, 13, 14, 16, 17, 30
  life reviews, 16, 17, 24, 30, 42
  lights, 13, 16, 17, 23, 26, 29, 32, 33, 35, 43
  music, 16, 26
  out-of-body feeling, 9, 12, 13, 16, 17, 23, 24, 26, 30, 33, 38, 41, 42
  peacefulness, 10, 16, 17, 18, 25, 26, 30, 32, 35, 38, 42
  previews of future, 17
  religious beings, 17, 21, 24, 32, 33, 34
  tunnels, 13, 17, 33
consciousness, 13–14
Cooper, Sharon, 41
definition of death, 12
Dostoyevsky, Fyodor, 42
dreams, 25, 41, 42, 45
drugs, 24–25, 42
epilepsy, 24, 42
French, Chris, 18, 24
Greyson, Bruce, 17, 23, 24, 27
Greyson Scale, 17
Heaven Is for Real, 34
Heim, Albert, 13
Hemingway, Ernest, 27, 34–35
hoaxes, 13, 34
Jung, Carl, 30
Junger, Sebastian, 33
Koch, Christof, 37
Lommel, Pim van, 30

Long, Jeffrey, 18, 24
MacArthur, John, 34
Madonna, 33–34
Malarkey, Alex, 34
Marsh, Michael N., 27
Monchaux, Pierre-Jean du, 29
Moody, Raymond, 23, 45
Nelson, Kevin, 37, 41
number of NDE survivors, 17, 21
Parnia, Sam, 9, 38, 41
Plato, 13, 29
post-NDEs, 25, 26, 27
Ring, Kenneth, 27, 41
Sagan, Carl, 23, 27
Saunders, George, 35
Schiefer, Randy, 33
scientific method, 23
scientific studies, 14, 17, 18, 19, 21, 23, 24, 37, 38, 41, 42
  AWARE, 38, 41
  Near-Death Experience Research Foundation (NDERF), 18
Shakespeare, William, 10, 45
  Hamlet, 10, 45
shared death experiences, 16
souls, 14, 19, 21, 29, 34
term origin, 14
terminal lucidity, 43
Tolkien, J. R. R., 35